Real S

WITHDRAWN   QUE S

D0258819

Raintree is an imprint of Capstone Global Library Limited, a company incorporated in England and Wales having its registered office at 7 Pilgrim Street, London, EC4V 6LB – Registered company number: 6695582

www.raintreepublishers.co.uk
myorders@raintreepublishers.co.uk

Edited by Rebecca Rissman, Daniel Nunn, and John-Paul Wilkins
Designed by Joanna Malivoire and Tim Bond
Picture research by Ruth Blair
Production by Sophia Argyris
Originated by Capstone Global Library Ltd
Printed and bound in China by South China Printing Company

ISBN 978 1 406 26351 0 (hardback)
17 16 15 14 13
10 9 8 7 6 5 4 3 2 1

ISBN 978 1 406 26358 9 (paperback)
18 17 16 15 14
10 9 8 7 6 5 4 3 2 1

British Library Cataloguing in Publication Data
Rissman, Rebecca.
Insects. – (Real size science)
571.3'157-dc23
A full catalogue record for this book is available from the British Library.

Acknowledgements
We would like to thank the following for permission to reproduce photographs: Getty Images p. 22 (photography by Evy Lipowski); Naturepl pp. 17 (© Bruce Davidson), 18 (© Robert Thompson); Shutterstock pp. 4 (© wagtail), 5 (© skynetphoto), 6 (© akkaradech), 7 (© Peeravit), 8 (© Subbotina Anna), 9 (© Henrik Larsson), 10 (© Sari ONeal), 11 top left (© Ainars Aunins), 11 top right, 19 (© Peter Reijners), 11 bottom left (© Erhan Dayi), 11 bottom right (© Donna Apsey), 12 (© LilKar), 13 (© Peter Wollinga), 14 (© irin-k), 15 (© Cosmin Manci), 16 (© Eric Isselee), 20 (© jps), 21 (© Marek R. Swadzba).

Cover photograph of a blue morpho butterfly perched on a leaf reproduced with permission of Shutterstock (© Brenda Carson).

We would like to thank Dee Reid and Nancy Harris for their invaluable help in the preparation of this book.

Every effort has been made to contact copyright holders of material reproduced in this book. Any omissions will be rectified in subsequent printings if notice is given to the publisher.

Contents

Different insects

There are many different types of insects.

Insects are different sizes.

Insects can be big.

rhinoceros beetle

Real size

looper

Real Size

Insects can be very small.

Insect body parts

All insects have three main body parts.

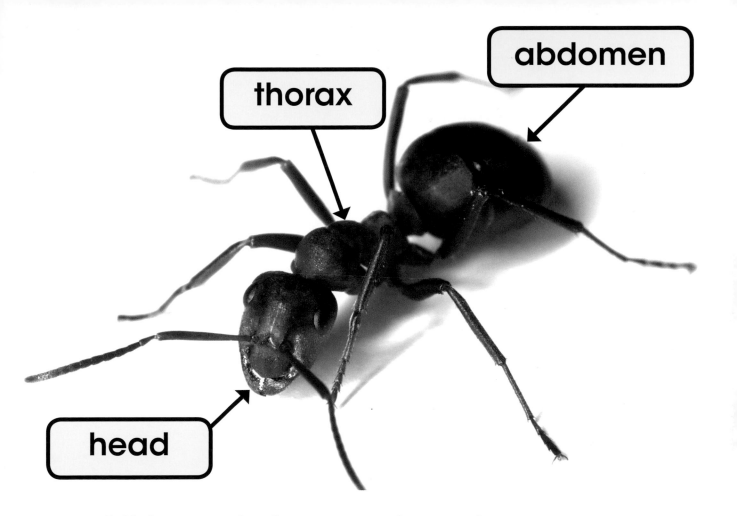

abdomen

thorax

head

All insects have a head,
a thorax, and an abdomen.

Wings

Some insects have wings.

Real Size

Wings help insects fly.

Honeybees are small insects.
Their wings are small.

Real size

Atlas moths are large insects.
Their wings are large.

Legs

All insects have six legs.

ladybird

flea

Insects' legs help them to move.

Crickets are small insects.
Their legs are small.

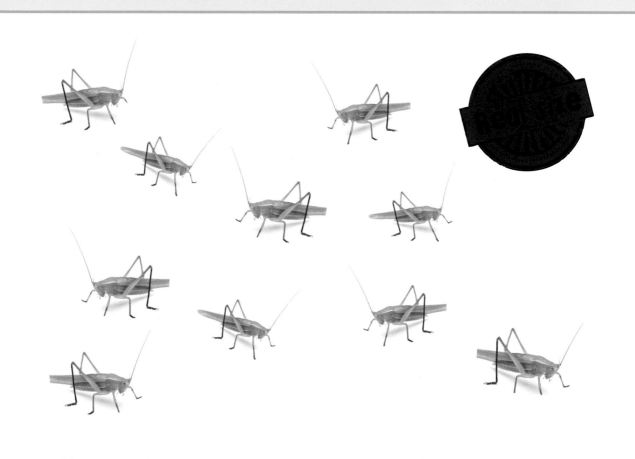

Real size

Goliath beetles are large insects.
Their legs are large.

Antennae

Antennae grow from insects' heads.

antennae

Real size

Real size

Antennae help insects to smell, taste, and touch.

Small copper butterflies have small antennae.

Real Size

Longhorn beetles have
large antennae.

Real size surprise!

The green darner is a large dragonfly.

This is its real size!

Real size

Picture glossary

abdomen third part of an insect's body

antennae body parts attached to an insect's head. Antennae help insects sense and move.

thorax middle part of an insect's body

Index

Notes for parents and teachers

Before reading
- Engage children in a discussion about insect sizes. Ask children to think of different ways we describe size, such as tall, short, wide, or thin.
- Tell children that we can use tools, such as rulers, to measure size. We can also use body parts, such as hand lengths and foot lengths, to measure size.

After reading
- Ask children to brainstorm a list of insects. Write them down on the board. Then encourage children to rank them in order of size. If you have any questions about how big some insects are, use this as an opportunity to show children how to safely look up this information on the internet.
- Turn to page 16. Ask children to measure the length of a cricket using a ruler.
- Turn to page 17. Ask children to measure the length of a goliath beetle using hand lengths (e.g., one hand length long, or half a hand length long).